They lived like this in
ANCIENT MEXICO

Author: MARIE NEURATH

Artist: JOHN ELLIS

of the Isotype Institute

FRANKLIN WATTS INC.

845 Third Avenue, New York 10022

© 1971 Isotype Institute Limited
Published by Franklin Watts Inc.,
845 Third Avenue, New York 10022, New York, U.S.A.
Printed by offset in Great Britain by
William Clowes and Sons, Limited, London, Beccles and Colchester
Library of Congress Catalog No. 71-147264
SBN 531 01395-2

ANCIENT MEXICO

Mexico is a land of many climates. To both east and west – on the Pacific coast and on the Gulf of Mexico – are narrow strips of land with tropical growth. Behind these, mountains rise sharply. Inland is a high plateau. A valley called the Valley of Mexico is part of this highland. The valley has rivers and lakes, and is surrounded by even higher mountains, some of whose peaks are covered in snow all the year round. The lakes were once much larger, and many ancient cities were built near them. This land was the heart of the Aztec civilisation.

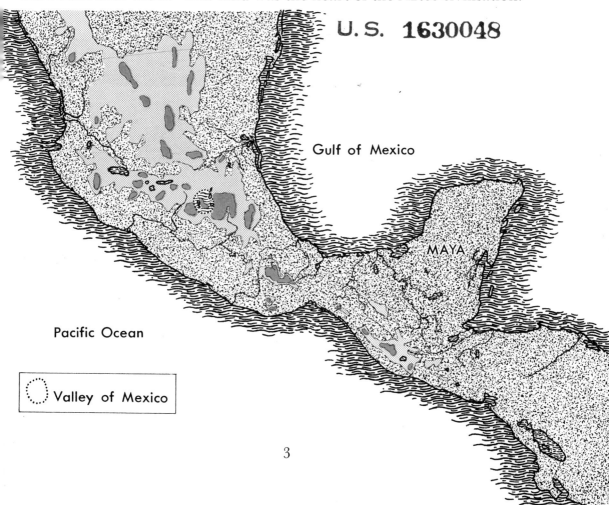

U. S. 1630048

Gulf of Mexico

MAYA

Pacific Ocean

Valley of Mexico

3

The first men had come to
America from Asia during
the Ice Ages. They reached
Mexico when that land was very
rainy and had many forests.

In these forests lived large animals such as tapirs, bison, and
mammoths. The men hunted them for food. Where they had their
meals they left many animal bones behind. On some of them they
scratched pictures of the animals they knew, like the one above.

When it became warmer, the ice melted in the north and there was less
rain in Mexico. Forests were replaced by grassland with such plants
as agave, cactus and yucca. The large forest animals died out.

Where isolated bits of forest remained,
only smaller animals lived on: monkeys,
for example, and an animal related to
the wild pig. There was little game
for hunters, so people had to move away
to find new sources of meat.

4

The people were good at catching wild water birds, like ducks, and later they learned to keep geese and turkeys. Some tribes had a special kind of hairless dog that they fattened for their meat.

The people went out in little boats to catch fish and shellfish. They knew many kinds in rivers, lakes and the sea. Painters drew them on the plates and bowls that the potters made.

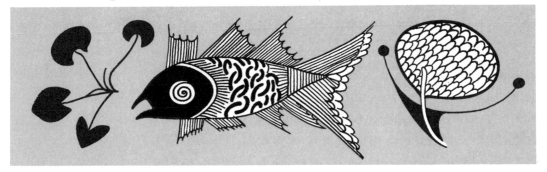

People hunted birds not only for their delicious meat, but even more for their bright feathers. They used blowpipes for bird hunting. This man has a stone in one hand and a pipe in the other. A bird with long curly feathers is above him in the tree.

The tree has pods on its stem. It is a cacao tree. These trees grew near the coasts in the tropical forests. The drink that the Mexicans made from the cacao beans was called chocolatl. It was a favourite drink, but only rich people could afford it. Each cacao bean was carefully kept. Often the beans served as money for the merchants.

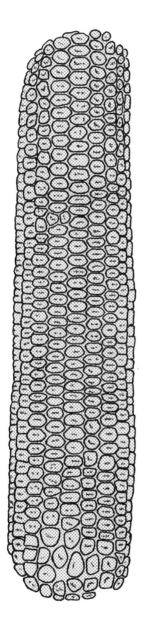

Mexico, with its wide range of climates, had a great variety of wild plants. The people knew them very well, and they were very good at finding plants suitable for cultivation in gardens and fields.
The most important of all was maize. As a wild Mexican plant it had only two seeds on each plant. Even when it was cultivated in ancient Mexico the cobs were tiny compared to present sizes, as shown here. But the food from even such small cobs was more reliable than any food the people had used before, and they thrived on it.

In addition, they grew squashes, beans, sweet potatoes (as shown in the symbol above, left), tomatoes, green and red peppers, pineapples and their beloved flowers (the flower symbol is above, right). Cactus leaves were also eaten. From the agave came a juice for an intoxicating drink, spikes for needles, and fibre for rough cloth and ropes. The people also cultivated cotton for making their clothes.

The cultivation of maize spread throughout the country, and there were villages everywhere. People built their huts near their plots; they made mats, clothes, and pots. They also made clay figures of men, boys, girls, and women. One of the women above carries a baby on her back. In an area near the Gulf coast people developed new skills. They could shape hard stone. This lively group was made by them. Near some stone slabs a number of men are standing together as if in a council meeting.

Some of the figures have strange faces –
half man, half jaguar. These were made
in many sizes – some gigantic, some small.
The one shown here is part of a stone axe,
which was found far away from the place
where it had been made. Much of this work
was carried to other regions; it must
have been very famous.

At the time of these artists, the first of
the great Mexican temples were built in
the same area. By now, priests and leaders
of the people must have played an important
part. Great ceremonies may have taken
place in the courtyards, with their walls and
mounds laid out before the temple.

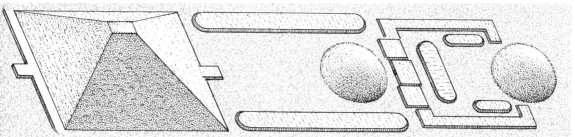

The temple itself was a large clay pyramid. Later Mexican temple
pyramids had a platform on top reached by a steep staircase. Hardly
ever were there tombs inside. The pyramids raised the place, where
sacrifice was offered to the gods, high above the people.

The early temple builders also played the famous ball game that spread throughout the country and even to the Mayan neighbours. The ball court was I-shaped: the wider ends were connected by a passage.

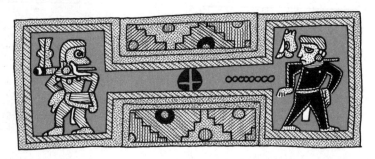

On the passage walls two stone rings were fixed. A hard ball of rubber that came from a tree that grew in the coastland forests was used. It had to be bounced through one of the rings, not with the hand, but with the hip. The men wore hard belts for this; they also protected their legs, as can be seen in the picture below. Here we can see something else: this was not just a game; a sacrifice was first made. Ball courts were in temple areas, and the ball game was one of the many ways in which sacrifice could be made to the gods.

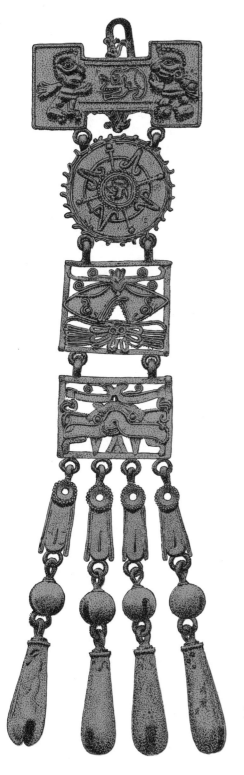

The top part of this gold ornament has the shape of a ball court. The two players are gods, and their ball is a skull.

The round ornament below is a symbol for the sun. The rectangular shapes underneath probably stand for the moon and the earth.

Perhaps it was believed that the ball game of the gods made the sun, the moon and the stars move in the skies.

There was nothing that the Mexicans feared more than that the sun should stop rising. They built temples and made blood sacrifices to urge the gods to go on giving them day and night, the seasons and the years, for ever.

11

For the farming people, the most
cherished god was the one who
gave them rain.

Here he is shown, surrounded by
his raindrops. He has a rather
frightening face that is hardly
human, with protruding teeth
and a curled nose. But he is a
friendly god. In the picture
below, his wife is sitting with
him near the lake of the earth.

The rain god was worshipped
everywhere from earliest times.
The greatest centre for his
worship was in the Valley of
Mexico, north of the lake.
Here were great pyramids of
the sun and the moon. Another
temple was decorated with faces
of the rain god, alternating
with faces of another great god:
the feathered serpent.

The feathered serpent was the god of wind, and also of knowledge.
Under his leadership, civilisation spread through the country. When
only his face was shown, it had its mouth open and showed rows of
sharp teeth. But this was not a frightening god, either. The times
were mostly peaceful. In the great town near the temple city the
people worked at many trades. They looked forward to a life after
death in the paradise of the rain god. A picture of this paradise,
with dancing people, butterflies and flowers, was painted on a wall
of one of the temples. Part of it is shown below.

This flourishing civilisation did not remain undisturbed for ever. Its fame spread, and attracted other people. In the north, simpler people lived the life of hunters and fishermen. They moved south and took possession of places where life was better. Other people followed and replaced their forerunners. Among the latest were the Aztecs. They found the best places occupied by stronger people. In the beginning they did not know where to settle.

This picture tells the old legend of how they sailed across a lake and found a cave. There their tribal god told them where to stay. They travelled by boat, they walked over land, as the footprints show, and listened to the words that came out of the mouth of the speaker in curly clouds. They later settled on an island in the lake in the Valley of Mexico.

The island on which they built their first huts was small. But very ingeniously they made it larger and larger until it became one of the most splendid towns of mankind. They called it Tenochtitlan, which means "At Cactus Rock". It was where Mexico City now is. What they did was this: in the shallow lake they collected mud and floating water plants into plots fenced in by basket work. They planted trees, and the roots locked the floating plots to the bottom of the lake. Each of the plots was allotted to a family group, some larger, others smaller. Between these islands were canals of clear water. The whole settled area was divided into four quarters by wider canals, crossed by a number of bridges. Traffic was by boat. There were footpaths, but no paved streets. Three solid causeways linked the island with the nearest shores – north, south and west. Fresh water was led from the hills in the west to the city centre.

The people worked their plots with sticks and without any animals to help them. Everybody grew maize. This could be stored for the winter in big jars; the kernels were picked from the cobs and sifted. For food, the kernels were ground into flour with a stone roller on a stone table.

Cooking and work were done out of doors. Aztec houses had one storey and flat mud-brick roofs. The houses served only as sleeping places. There were mats to lie or sit on. Only richer people had legless seats with a support for the back.

Nearly all of Tenochtitlan was built of lava stone. The centre of the town, based on the rock of the original island, was the only part that could carry heavy buildings. The palaces of the ruling families were there. They had platforms, staircases, and many rooms. In one of the rooms of the chief's palace a council used to sit to deal with court cases.

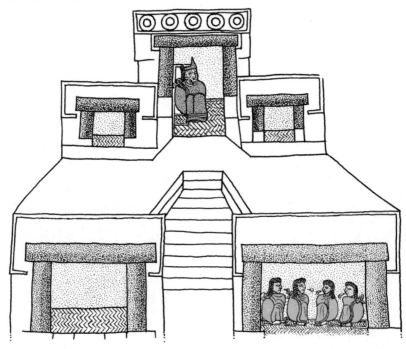

The most important buildings in any town were the temple pyramids. Often these were built in such a way that people near the bottom could not see the top, and the staircase seemed to lead up into the sky. Only from a distance could one see that the temple on top often had a high and decorated roof.

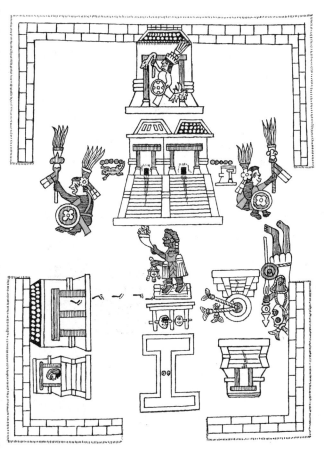

In the centre of Mexico City there were twin temple pyramids. One was dedicated to the rain god, the other to the god of sun and of war, who was the Aztecs' special god.

A priest standing in the centre of the square has come, as the footprints show, from his quarters at the left. Below him are a skull rack and a ball court. There were more temples for other gods.

The priests had a busy life, and not a very pleasant one. They had to provide enough sacrifices for the hungry gods. They had to prick their skin often, to give their own blood. They painted themselves black all over and never cut their hair, and were a rather horrible sight. One of their main responsibilities was to make sure that the day and the time of day were right for any activity. There were many unlucky days and hours. If somebody was born on an unlucky day, the name-giving at least had to take place on a lucky one.

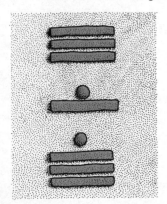

For every event of importance the exact date was recorded. That is why many of the oldest stone monuments carry the symbols for a date. Dots stand for number 1, lines for 5. Sometimes a finger is used for number 1, as in the second picture.

There were various ways of fixing a date. Among them was the usual calendar year of 365 days, which the Mexicans, who watched the sky, knew very well. They had 18 months of 20 days, and 5 extra days, which were unlucky. Besides this, they had a sacred year, based on their sacred number, 13. The numbers 1 to 13 were combined with 20 different day symbols; the 260 possible combinations made up the sacred year.

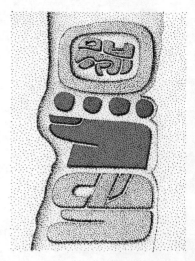

In the first two rows, 10 day symbols are combined with numbers 1 to 10: crocodile, wind, house, lizard, serpent; death's head, deer, rabbit, water, dog.

Day symbols monkey, grass, reed follow for numbers 11 to 13. The next 2 symbols, ocelot (a wild cat) and eagle, get the numbers 1 and 2 again.

The last 5 symbols, vulture, motion, flint knife, rain, and flower, are combined with numbers 3 to 7. Then the first 5 symbols follow again.

But now crocodile, wind, house, lizard, serpent are combined with 8 to 12. Only after 13 repeats will the same combinations reappear.

19

The Mexicans were afraid that time might come to a dead stop. The end
of an old year and the beginning of a new one was a dangerous break.
Usually their two kinds of year had different breaks, and the one
helped the other along. Once every 52 years, however, the sacred year
ended at the same time as the calendar year. During the night when
this happened, all the people would be up to watch whether the sky
went on revolving. All fires had to be put out, all pots destroyed.

Nor were the priests idle. They did everything, according to their
age-old rules, to bring about a new beginning. They offered sacrifices
to the gods, and over the chest of a man who had given his blood, they
turned their sacred sticks in the holes of a wooden board to start a
new fire. They proved the power of their rituals when they succeeded
in making the sun rise again, to everybody's great relief. Now life
could go on. All fires were rekindled; new pots were made.

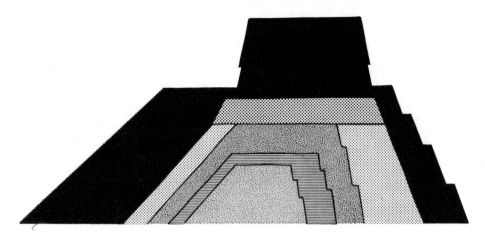

Even the temple pyramids had to be renewed. They were covered all over, and a larger pyramid was built over the old one. Many layers have been found at certain important places, and mostly they follow each other in 52-year intervals.

When a new temple was dedicated, more sacrifices were required. The chief god of the Aztecs, the god of war and sun, needed more blood than any other before. Mostly, prisoners of war served for sacrifice. The man in the picture, whose feet are bound to a heavy stone, is a war prisoner. Many Aztec wars had no other purpose but taking prisoners who could be sacrificed.

Whether the Aztecs could have grown into gentler habits nobody can tell. They did not get a chance: their life was cut short by the Spanish conquerors. At that time they were becoming a literate people. Books, written by the priests, were made at many places.

This is how they recorded the death of a king and the succession of another at a certain date. The year is "Twelve Rabbit". The names of the kings are "Smoky Shield" and "Snake of Knives".

Sheets of paper were made from bark that was beaten flat and smooth. Most of the painted books were based on thin bands of deer skin that was covered by a white coating. The bands were folded.

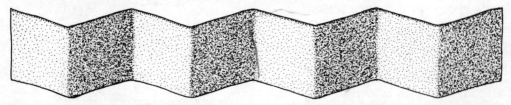

The Aztecs had signs that represented certain things. They used them to stand for these things, and also for names that had a similar sound.

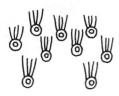  

These are the signs for rain, for water, and for gold.

This symbol combines an arm and a
hand with the signs for water and
for gold. It means "the place where
you can find gold in the water".

In the same way, the names of the kings on the previous page have been
put together. The first king's name, in Aztec, sounded like "Smoky
Shield". The signs for "shield" and "smoke" are therefore combined.

 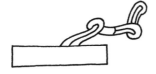 

In the same way, "snake" and "knives" are combined for the second name.

The mass of the people led their lives undisturbed by the worries and
pursuits of priests and warriors. They perfected their crafts of making
pots and clay figures, carving wood or piercing stone beads to string
them together. Their most valued stones were turquoise and jade, symbols
of the bright sun and the fertile earth. The people used obsidian
which came from the volcanoes around Tenochtitlan. It was hard and
could be worked into sharp blades or polished into shining mirrors.

The people collected the most colourful feathers for the decoration
of headgear and shields. For the shields they first made the shape in
basketwork, as shown in the last picture.

 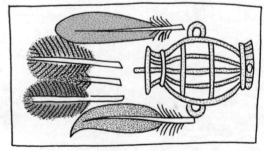

Weaving was women's work. The rich people wore cloth woven in many colours and patterns. Materials for women's tunics were often also embroidered.

At first on the west coast, later everywhere in Mexico, there were goldsmiths. Probably the Mexicans learned goldwork from the people in Panama, with whom they were in contact through boat travel along the Pacific coast. Gold was melted and cast in moulds. It was also made into thin sheets, which were then shaped and hammered. Gold ornaments were worn in the ears, the lower lip, and the nose.

The earlobes, lower lips and nose had to be pierced to carry their ornaments. Here such an operation on the nose can be seen.

25

The Aztecs built a great dam to separate their sweet-water lake from the rest of the large lake, which became more and more salty. But besides their three causeways between island and shores, they built no roads. People had no carts and no animals to carry their loads. They either went by boat, or they carried their loads on their backs.

They placed the strips of their backloads over their forehead and moved along with short, running steps, as Mexicans still do today. Carriers were often volunteers who went on trading journeys for adventure. Others went with the merchants who planned the journey to earn a living. There were poor people. Some were so poor that they sold themselves to secure food and shelter for their families. Slaves all had to wear wooden collars.

Strangely enough, some Mexicans had the idea of using a wheel, but only for toys, which have been unearthed. Wheels and carts for transport came to America only with the Europeans.

In the markets, the goods were pleasantly displayed, as they are today in Mexico. There were special markets for food, others for household goods. The merchants made long journeys with their carriers to bring special goods to the markets of the capital city. In exchange, they offered goods from the highlands.

Among the highland products were cloth, tunics, gold ornaments, copper ware, obsidian tools, and ropes made from the fibre of agave.

Among the tropical products were shells, jaguar skins, cacao, jade beads and feathers.

The merchants knew more about foreign countries than anybody else did. They were useful to the ruler, because they could tell him the best places from which to get tribute. This king, with shield and spear thrower, is dressed for war, with his helmet of an animal's face.

A king had to go out with his army from time to time, to get prisoners. How much more useful to find some wealth, too. This is the symbol for the conquest of a town: a weapon stuck into a rocklike shape. When a town was captured, its temples were burned and the images of the gods and sacred books were taken away or burned.

Young men were trained to fight with clubs studded with obsidian blades. They also learned to shoot arrows. Their headgear showed whether they were good soldiers and had taken prisoners.

feathers

royal headgear

cochineal dye

blanket

shield

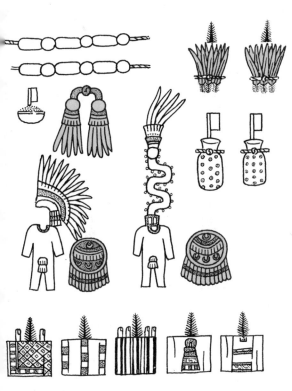

Tribute was stored, and records were kept in which number signs were combined with signs for things. The haul recorded here contains:
2 strings of jade beads,
20 bowls of gold dust,
800 bunches of feathers,
40 bags of cochineal dye,
2 warrior's costumes,
402, 400, 404, 400, 400 blankets of various patterns. The number 8,000 does not occur here, but in the picture on page 21, where the number 20,000 is represented by two symbols for 8,000 and ten symbols for 400.

I   20 $20 \times 20 = 400$ 404 $400 \times 20 = 8,000$

There were special schools for the training of priests and soldiers. Mostly the boys came from the same group of families; their fathers had been trained in the same way. But a poor boy could also enter school if he was highly gifted or had distinguished himself otherwise. All other children received their education at home.

Girls had to learn to clean, cook, spin, and weave. This girl is being instructed how to spin. She gets $1\frac{1}{2}$ loaves a day, as she is under 11.

Boys had to learn to work the field and the garden, to work wood and stone, to paddle a boat, and to catch fish. This boy is being taught to use a fishing net.

Punishments, too, were different for boys and girls. While admonitions were given, a girl was pricked with sharp thorns from the agave plant, and a boy had to breathe in the sharp fumes from a fire of peppers.

For entertainment at court there
were jugglers and musicians,
dwarfs and hunchbacks.

Drums and rattles accompanied
the singing. There were pipes
and shells to blow on, and
gongs with just two different
notes. There was more rhythm
than melody in music making.

There were toys for children
and festivals for the people.
There were board games and sports.

This man fights as a gladiator,
but he cannot win. He is a
prisoner of war on a sacrificial
stone, surrounded by his captors.

The Aztecs believed that there was no better death than to offer oneself to the gods and enter the paradise of the war god for eternal bliss. Wars gave them this chance. In their wars they did not go out to destroy. Only when the Europeans arrived did they learn of another type of war, that brought utter destruction. All kingdoms were wiped out, most towns and temples razed to the ground.

At first, the Spaniards were welcomed because they had horses and shining armour and seemed to be gods. But the friendly encounter ended in total war, defeat, and humiliation. Churches were built on the rubble of pyramids. The memory of old times was to be entirely erased. Only a few priests took an interest in the Aztecs and made their artists draw pictures of their former life. Today the Mexicans have turned back to their past and rediscovered what their forefathers achieved.